MW01601534

Man and

Wife

Unholy Matrimony

A novella by Andrelle Leandre

A goal without a plan is just a wish

~ Antoine de Saint-Exupéry ~

Dedication

In the loving memory of my mother, Elcie, and my brother, Ferranti, who could not be here to share this amazing accomplishment with me. I dedicate this book to you both. I hope I can continue to honor your memories and allow your unforgettable spirits to live on through my work.

I would also like to dedicate this book to my son, Dion. I hope that writing this book will help me establish a better future for you, my love. I also hope that this will motivate you to chase your own dreams someday, because life is truly meant to be lived.

Acknowledgement

I am proud to finally conclude my first published story. This marks a monumental milestone in my life, and I would like to acknowledge a few people who always encouraged me to finish what I started.

Leana "Lea" Jean-Francois has been a member of my family since her mother married my uncle. Lea was always willing to be the personal proofreader for my stories since we were children. Kolleen Francis has been my best friend since the age of thirteen and has always supported me chasing my dreams. I shared every detail of this experience with her and although our friendship is long-distance, the support I received from her is felt closely. Finally, Darrion Lewis is my boyfriend and the father of my son, whose overwhelming belief in my talent gave me the confidence to take the big step of getting this story published.

Also, I would like to acknowledge the hardest working man I know, my father Ferere Leandre. I would like to honor him and show appreciation for him going above and beyond to support his family for over 30 years. I am grateful to have him as a father and even more grateful that he helped me invest in this project. Although I could never repay him for all that he has done for me, I hope that this acknowledgement will serve as a small gesture of my undying gratitude.

In summation, I wish I could list every single person in my life that inspired me to take this step as an aspiring author. My cousins Reginald, Renald, Leana and Jeff also acted as powerhouses of ideas on how to become successful by chasing dreams. Without the constant motivation from my loved ones, the completion of this story would not have been possible.

Thank you all.

Synopsis

In 1969, gender roles in the small town of Huntley, Illinois were very clear; men worked, and women stayed home with the kids. Diane Sutton had devoted her life to being a wife and mother. That all changes when her husband Frank is involved in a serious car crash, and she must assume the role of breadwinner.

Diane's new career opens her eyes and her mind to new things, but will her husband be able to handle Diane's new attitude when he returns home? How far will Frank go to maintain dominance over his wife? Meanwhile, the decline of their marriage begins to take its toll on their teenaged daughter, Lori.

Table of Contents

Chapter 1

A Woman's Place

February 1969

It was a calm Monday morning in the Sutton residence. Frank Sutton, the patriarch of the family, was woken up by a symphony of birds chirping. He started his day with a cup of Folgers: black with three teaspoons of sugar. The aroma of coffee brewing filled up the two-bedroom home as the other members of the household awakened as well.

The village of Huntley, Illinois was a very small and religious town less than an hour West of Chicago. The Sutton family lived in a tight-knit, suburban community composed mostly of middle-class white families and just a handful of African Americans. Racial tensions were moderate, and it was a peaceful community overall. This morning, Frank got up earlier than usual and sat in the den to make a phone call. He wound back the rotary phone to dial the numbers and spoke in a hushed tone when he got an answer.

Frank's 15-year-old daughter was walking through the hall when she overheard her father's conversation.

"Dad?" she asked while rubbing the slumber out of her eyes.

"I'll speak to you later," Frank said while rushing off the phone. "Yes, doll. What are you doing up so early?"

"I just needed to use the bathroom." She responded.

"Okay. I'm off to work, doll." Frank said before hastily heading out the front door.

The Sutton family had two vehicles: a new Buick in pristine condition, which was primarily Frank's car, and an old station wagon his wife would use to do market runs, drive to church, and take their daughter to school. The lawn was still damp from morning dew and the stench of rain from the night before was still potent in the morning air. Frank squinted at the intense glare from the rising sun while adjusting the visor as he merged onto the highway. Forty-two-year-old Frank Sutton was a floor supervisor at the local auto parts plant, and he was well respected and slightly feared in his workplace. He had black hair, a thin mustache and a wide jaw that hardened his already unsociable face.

An hour later, Lorena Sutton sat at the breakfast table, putting the finishing touches on her history assignment.

"Shouldn't that homework already have been completed, young lady?" Her mother asked as she set a plate of eggs and bacon on the table in front of Lorena.

"I would have finished it sooner, but I spent most of the weekend with…" Lorena stifled the rest of her statement.

"With whom, Lori"?

"No one. I just got a little distracted, mom, that's all."

"Lori, we talked about this already. If you're going to have a boyfriend, your father and I need to meet him. Bring him over for supper sometime."

Diane let Lori get away with dating her boyfriend before being introduced to the family for long enough, she was anxious to meet the boy her daughter was so smitten with.

Like many other women in her community, Diane Sutton was a stay-at-home wife and mother; she assumed the household responsibilities while Frank worked full-time and handled the finances. She met Frank right out of high school, they married when she turned 19, and she gave birth to their daughter two years later.

During the early years of her marriage, Diane was eager to live up to society's expectations of being "the perfect wife". A woman's value was essentially based on how clean she could keep her home and how well she knew her way around the kitchen. Wondrous and imaginative, she would sometimes stare out the living-room window and stalk the neighbors as they walked up and down the street. She watched her neighbors and wondered about them, about their lives, what kind of people they were and what kind of work they did, etc. When her imagination would get restless, she would grab a notebook and a pen and write short stories. At that time, there wasn't much for a young, new mother to do; she did not have many friends and her made-up tales of fiction amused her.

These days, Diane spent most of her time sifting through home shopping catalogs, looking to fill her house with the latest gizmos and gadgets or socializing with other housewives in the neighborhood. She recently charged a new blender and vacuum to Frank's credit card to add to her collection of nifty accessories. Diane was growing tired of television; she thought she would lose her mind if she had to sit through another Julia Child cooking segment. She had attempted Beef wellington, souffles and a few other recipes to keep her occupied.

She was engraved into her regular routine of cooking, cleaning, and doing laundry. A part of her had felt empty for a long time. She had a nice house, a color television set, and a husband that paid all the bills. Why wasn't that enough?

That same afternoon, Diane was in desperate need of company and had her best friend Betty Morris over along with Barbara Ross, a local housewife Diane knew from the community. Diane shared the rocky state of her marriage with the ladies in hopes of getting some helpful advice in return.

"Our relationship has been suffering lately. Frank seems distant and uninterested." Diane prayed for God to give her the tools to be a better wife.

"Maybe you two should have another baby," Barbara suggested.

"I don't know about that. You remember how my last pregnancy ended," Diane stated. Back in 1960, she had learned that she was pregnant with her second child, a boy this time. She spent the first few weeks of her pregnancy daydreaming about what the handsome little fella would have looked like or if he would grow up to be a successful athlete or a businessman. He was rambunctious and filled with energy even in the womb; he began kicking early at 12 weeks, which started off feeling like little flutters that gradually grew stronger each day. Ten weeks later, Diane noticed the baby stopped kicking, and later, she began hemorrhaging blood. The doctors had to break the news that Diane was suffering from a miscarriage. Her son would have been eight years old this year.

"Don't let that discourage you. You're still young. Nothing brings a couple closer than a new bundle of joy." Barbara spoke with confidence.

"A baby isn't going to fix your problems, Diane. It seems like you're the only one trying to better this marriage. Why does all the responsibility of improving your relationship have to fall on your shoulders? Frank should put in the work, too." Betty pointed out.

"How can you say that, Betty? Between working hard every day and paying all the bills, men don't have time to worry themselves with issues like this." Barabara believed that the solution to Diane's issue was contingent on how much she catered to her husband.

"All I'm saying is that if Frank doesn't want to treat you better, then you don't need him." Betty always had her reservations about Frank; she knew how ruthless he could be and often worried about Diane's safety. There was a particular incident that left a lasting impression on Betty about Frank and soured any chance of them ever having a cordial relationship.

"Oh, Betty, don't put such thoughts in her head. Diane might lose her husband."

"I suppose that would be a shame. How in the world would she go on?" Betty's statement was riddled with sarcasm. Diane was beginning to regret inviting these two ladies to her home; she should have known their opposite personalities would eventually clash.

Barbara scowled at Betty before excusing herself from the Sutton residence, "I really should be going. I have got to get home to my husband. Betty, you wouldn't understand."

As soon as the door shut, Diane asked, "Betty, why do you always have to do that?"

"Do what?"

"Argue! It's not lady-like. You keep up that attitude, and no man will ever have you," Diane warned.

"There are scarier things in the world than being single." Betty Morris was Diane's plus-sized, confident, and single gal pal. Betty always said if God had intended for her to get married, he would've given her more patience and a smaller waistline. She adopted the principles of feminism, and she was a bad influence on Diane, according to Frank.

Lori was the it-girl at school, she thrived in academics, participated in activities, and was adored by her teachers. She strolled through the halls with her books pressed up against her chest as her bouncy, blonde hair dangled above her shoulders. Lori wore a green turtleneck sweater, black pants, and close-toed flats shoes. She eventually bumped into Andrew Wilson; a gorgeous, green-eyed sophomore Lori had a thing for. Drew was nearly 6 feet tall and usually had on at least one article of leather clothing at any given time. His dark brown hair was gelled back with one strand curled in the front like a 50's greaser.

"I had fun this past weekend." Drew said before gently grabbing Lori's hand. She noticed how his dimples were indented on his cheeks when he smiled.

Lori grinned and said, "So did I. That movie was far out." Lori and Drew had spent Saturday night at the drive-in; they cuddled in the back seat of his Volkswagen van and watched a horror movie, munching on popcorn and sugary snacks. The pair stood by the lockers and recalled their favorite scenes from the slasher film.

"By the way, my parents want to meet you," Lori mentioned.

"Yeah, I'm cool with that. You don't look too happy about it, though. Should I be nervous?" Drew asked, slightly concerned."

"Well, my dad is unfriendly and unapproachable, and my mom acts like a mindless puppet that pretty much goes along with whatever he says. Other than that, we're your typical American family." Lori said cynically with a fake smile.

"Okay, whatever you say," he smirked before making plans to be there tomorrow at 7:30 pm.

"That works, I'll let my mom know."

"See you then, beautiful." Drew winked at her before making his way through the halls.

As dinner started that same evening, the Suttons gathered around their dining room table with empty stomachs, ready to dig in. Diane was an excellent cook; she prepared a savory pot roast, red potatoes and sautéed string beans. Each bite was more flavorful than the last. Diane slid a Marlboro menthol in her mouth and proceeded to light it, but Frank snatched the cigarette from between her lips before she even had a chance to. "You know I hate that," Frank snarled at Diane, as he could not stand the smell of smoke in the house.

"How was work, honey?" She started their routine conversations.

"Not great, our sales are down 15% this quarter since that foreign auto parts factory opened in Evanston.

Diane posed, "Why is that"?

"We can't compete with those damn foreign cars; they last just as long as American-made cars, and their parts cost a third of the price. Anyways, how was your day?" Frank had something new and interesting to talk about every day after work, unlike his wife, whose humdrum days were filled with repetitive and tedious tasks.

"Same old, same old. I did some housework, two loads of laundry and caught the end of *Gilligan's Island*. However, I did run into Phyllis Thompson at the market this weekend, and she said she is starting a new job as a telephone operator. Isn't that exciting?"

"Phyllis Thompson? Isn't that Ted's wife?" Frank asked, confused at why a married woman would need an occupation.

"Ex-wife honey, they've been divorced almost a year now."

Frank chuckled while taking another forkful of pot roast, "Well, no wonder she is working. She's divorced with no man to provide for her; now she has to fend for herself." He continued to say, "Don't go letting Phyllis fill your head with all these silly ideas of working. You don't need a job; you have a husband who takes care of you." Lori's eyes followed her parents as they went back and forth.

Diane explained, "I disagree, Frank. I think working is good for a lady's self-esteem. I find it liberating." Lori smiled at her mother's comment.

Frank raised his voice across the dinner table, "Enough, Diane! Phyllis having to work is not liberating! It's the consequence of a failed marriage." Frank bellowed arrogantly; the last thing he needed was Diane even considering that a woman could survive without a man in her life.

The thunder of Frank's voice quickly silenced Diane, and Lori sighed with disappointment as her mother's inspiring display of self-expression came to a swift end.

Lori had noticed that her parents had issues in their relationship and tried to see things from both of their points of view, but she wished her mom would stand up to her father more often.

"Diane, I'll be away on business this weekend; I have a meeting with the regional manager in Milwaukie. I'll be leaving on Thursday." Frank said as he removed his reading glasses before bed.

"Okay," Diane responded. Frank took business trips like this a few times a year, yet another exciting aspect of having a career, which she longed for. "Good luck with the meeting." She kissed her husband goodnight and turned off her bedside lamp before receding under the covers.

The next day, Diane planned to tackle the basement downstairs, which was long overdue for a cleanup. The basement housed old clothes, toys Lori grew out of and holiday decorations. She consolidated items into smaller boxes, dusted the moderately cobwebbed shelves and disposed of junk that hadn't been used in years. She used a step ladder to get a better look at the top shelf of the storage rack, where she came across a silver metal box. She stepped down from the ladder with the dusty lockbox in her hand. It was small, about eight inches wide and much heavier than it looked. This was bizarre; whatever was in this box must have contained something important enough to be under lock and key, but if it was so important, what was it doing forgotten in the basement? These questions only further aroused her suspicion.

Diane stared at the tiny keyhole in the front of the box and wondered what she could use to open it. She headed up to the kitchen and searched through the drawers for something to make that box ajar. She found an old screwdriver and tried to pry the box open, but it was no use. When she finally exhausted herself, she put the box away until she was ready to go at it again.

Later that evening, Drew arrived at 1304 South Maple Drive. The house had a long driveway and a garage. The home was standard-size, and there were tall, forest-like trees in the front yard. It looked like the kind of place where people might hunt deer in the winter. The walk to this front door seemed endless; suddenly, his palms were sweaty, and his throat was dry. Nervousness began to build up inside of him as this was his first time formally meeting a girl's parents, but even as apprehensive as he was, he knew Lori was worth it. A few knocks on the door later, Diane opened it, and Drew introduced himself.

"Good evening, Mrs. Sutton. I am Andrew Wilson, Lori's friend."

"Hello Andrew, we've been expecting you. Come on in," Diane pleasantly welcomed him and led them to the living room. Would you care for something to drink?" She offered, and Drew asked for a glass of water.

"Kids, help yourselves to some dinner rolls. We can start dinner once Mr. Sutton arrives." Dinner could not start without the man of the house present, so Lori and Drew made themselves comfortable on the couch and watched tv in the meantime.

When Frank finally arrived, Diane had a few questions regarding his whereabouts.

"Where have you been, dear? I was worried."

"I made a stop after work."

"Where did you go?" Diane asked, curious to know what was taking up so much of his time.

Frank became defensive and replied with, "I grabbed a couple of drinks after my shift and ended up staying a little longer than I planned. Are you through with your little questionnaire?"

"I was just concerned about what was taking you so long to get here." Diane could feel Frank's hostility growing.

"What do you want from me, Diane? I work hard, I pay the bills, and I come home to you every night. It's not your place to question me about where I am or what I'm doing."

Lori and Drew sat at the table, waiting to be served as they could hear Frank and Diane's quarrel. Lori sunk deeper into her chair, embarrassed by her parents' constant bickering.

Defeated, Diane dropped the conversation and proceeded to the dining room to serve supper. Dinner went smoothly for the most part. Drew turned his head occasionally, attempting to sneak a peek at Lori's chest, which seemed to poke out of her sweater that night. Frank barely spoke; he vaguely introduced himself to Drew, and he didn't seem to be very interested in getting to know him at all. Diane chattered on, trying her best to distract Drew from noticing Frank's rudeness, but it didn't work.

On Thursday, Diane and Lori met Frank in the driveway to bid him farewell before he hit the road. "Have a safe trip, honey," Diane said before giving him a peck on the lips.

"See you soon, dad."

"Good-bye, doll. Listen to your mother while I'm gone."

The ladies waved to Frank as he backed into the street and drove off. They entered the house and exchanged relieved looks with each other.

A few days later, Frank was on his way home from his business trip during a terrible thunderstorm. The rain pummeled his windshield, and another car abruptly stopped in front of him. As the vehicles got closer and closer to each other, Frank desperately slammed his foot on the brakes in an effort to avoid hitting the cars before him. Instead of slowing down, the tires just slid over the wet pavement. Frank swerved the steering wheel, and the slick road sent his Buick flying off the freeway and into a ditch. The sedan flipped twice before landing and the side of his car rammed into a tree, which caused the windshield to shatter. Shards of broken glass left incisions all over his arms and hands. The impact of the wreck caused the airbag to be deployed instantly and smash against his face. A bystander saw the accident and exited the highway to use a payphone and call 911.

Hours later, Diane became worried sick about Frank, who was still not home yet from Milwaukee. "That's funny. Frank should have been home by now." She declared while using a rag to dry off the wet dishes in the sink.

"I'm sure he's fine," Lori said, unbothered as she laid on the couch and flipped through the latest issue of Cosmo magazine.

After hearing a few knocks on the front door, Diane stopped what she was doing and proceeded to open it. There was a man standing on her porch, dressed in a brown sports-coat and a black hat.

"Hello." She greeted the stranger kindly.

"Hello, is this the Sutton residence?"

"Yes. I'm Diane Sutton."

"May I come in? This situation is regarding your husband, Frank." The man informed her.

"Of course," she welcomed him in and led him to the living room. "Please have a seat. My husband should have arrived from a business trip hours ago, but I never heard from him. Is he alright?" Diane asked, growing nervous.

"How rude of me, madam, I didn't introduce myself. I am Officer Greene with the Chicago Police Department. Mrs. Sutton, it is my regret to inform you that your husband was involved in a serious car crash on interstate 94."

"What?" Diane squealed as her hands trembled.

"He was transported to St. Ramone's Medical center. I hear he is in critical condition."

Diane quickly grabbed her purse and locked up before she and Lori immediately raced over to the hospital.

Chapter 2

Revelation

Frank was rushed to the hospital. He occasionally heard the sounds of muffled voices and an ambulance siren as he would drift in and out of consciousness. Paramedics swung open the ambulance doors as emergency staff arrived swiftly to wheel him to the trauma center. Nurses placed Frank's bruised and battered body from the gurney onto the hospital bed. Scissors were used to cut the shirt right off his torso before he was intubated and hooked up to an IV.

Frank was barely conscious but still breathing; he could feel the illumination from fluorescent hospital lights behind his closed eyelids. Once Frank was stabilized, the doctor ordered everything from ultrasounds to x-rays to check for internal bleeding and any broken bones. Frank began to wake up a short while later in his own private room. He slowly opened his eyes to see the silhouette of a short, pear-shaped woman. All he could remember since the crash was feeling an immeasurable amount pain in his leg.

"Where am I? What is going on?" Frank asked, his voice weakened.

The nurse had just returned to check Frank's vitals and monitor his progress. "Hello, Mr. Sutton. I am nurse Simmons, and you are at St. Ramone's hospital. You suffered many injuries from a car crash," she explained while jotting down a few notes onto her clipboard.

"Has my wife been notified?" Frank asked as he slowly regained awareness.

"The authorities did inform your wife. She should be here soon. The doctor will be in shortly to discuss further details," she verbalized before quietly exiting the room.

The doctor arrived a few moments later, looked over Frank's x-ray results and said, "You're lucky to be alive, Frank. You suffered a broken leg, three fractured ribs, and a concussion." The doctor also explained that his treatment plan would include surgery followed by a few months of intensive physical therapy.

The conversation was interrupted by the sound of the door opening. In walked Diane and Lori.

"Dad are you okay?" Lori bellowed with relief.

Diane approached Frank slowly. Seeing him lying on a hospital bed was somber, yet a darker, more sick part of Diane got the slightest bit of satisfaction from seeing her husband in that condition. It was strange to see someone so domineering in such a vulnerable position; it made him seem more human.

"I'm a little banged up, doll. They say I need surgery." Frank winced with pain from Lori's tight embrace.

"Is that really necessary?" Diane asked, concerned about Frank going under the knife.

Frank signed some consent forms giving the hospital permission to operate on him, and his surgery took place later that evening. The procedure was a success; Frank had a full cast on his right leg and bandages wrapped around his abdomen. The doctor articulated, "We will begin treatment once your bones have healed."

Even with Frank in the hospital, Diane was attentive and nurturing; she fluffed his pillows, brought him home-cooked meals, and tried to make his stay at the hospital as comfortable as possible. "Here is a list of things I'll need during my stay," Frank uttered the next day without a 'please' or 'thank you'. He requested his toiletries from home, a crossword puzzle, and a radio for easy listening.

A few weeks later, Betty invited Diane out for lunch at a restaurant by the pier. The ladies talked over drinks while eyeing the menu. Betty was a successful cosmetics saleswoman; she worked, traveled, and casually dated younger men. She truly lived her life to the fullest.

They got along well—however, their values differed. Diane sought fulfillment by being a devoted wife and mother, and Betty sought fulfillment from her own personal interests, not based on the needs of others. The unlikely pair met at the annual block party a few years ago and hit it off; they had been best friends ever since. Frank couldn't stand Betty and called her 'the lesbian'; he was convinced that Betty was secretly in love with Diane and wanted her all to herself. Diane would brush off his ridiculous theory and say that he was just being paranoid.

"How is Frank's recovery coming along?" Betty asked—not because she cared but because it was polite.

"Not quick enough. The other day at the market, Frank's credit card declined. I don't know how much longer we can go on like this. I'm afraid if he doesn't get better soon, we might lose the house."

"So, get a job in the meantime," Betty suggested.

"Betty, I couldn't possibly do that. You know how traditional Frank is."

"Don't be so old-fashioned; we're teetering on the brink of a new decade. Lots of women have jobs now." Betty stated before taking a bite from her club sandwich.

"Frank's ego would never allow me to work. He would rather I burn through our savings, but these bills aren't going to pay themselves."

"Well, it's not really Frank's decision, Diane. Your husband is in a hospital bed. If you're serious about finding work, I could talk to someone I know and maybe get you a job at his office. The job doesn't pay much, but it's better than nothing."

"I don't know about this." Diane had never needed to make such decisions before; it was overwhelming just to think about it—working, paying the bills, and keeping up with the household chores.

"It's either that or living on the streets," Betty said while sipping her martini. Diane shook her head in agreement and took Betty up on her offer.

24

Not long after, Betty was able to pull some strings and land Diane a job as a secretary with *Suncoast Ventures*, a small business only 15 minutes away from her home. Since Frank's Buick was wrecked in the car crash, the Sutton family was down to one car. As she drove the old, beat-up station wagon, the rusty bolts in the doors would make a squeaky noise when opening or shutting, and it always took a few tries to get the engine running.

Despite the bumpy ride, Diane arrived early, and she was shown around the office by the owner of the company, Lou Livingston. Lou was an overweight and ill-mannered brute.

"Listen up, Toots, you're in charge of answering the phones, sorting and filing paperwork," Lou said in a raised tone, with a mouth full of food.

"It's Diane," she responded.

"Huh?"

"My name. It's Diane."

"Yea, yea, sure it is, Toots." Lou ignored her effort to correct him. "You'll also be responsible for writing and sending out letters to our clients regarding their policy," Lou explained as he led her to a small file room with a typewriter.

25

She marveled at the steel, powder blue beauty. She always wanted to get one of her own but being a housewife, mother and now a full-time secretary wouldn't leave much room for writing.

When Diane arrived home, she kicked off her heels and threw Frank's keys onto the kitchen table. She flopped onto the couch and watched the ceiling fan spin around in circles. She rubbed her forehead, exhausted from work with a pile of dirty dishes waiting for her in the sink. She kept asking herself if starting a career was the right decision.

Diane showed up to work on time every day and completed all the tasks given to her. Two weeks later, she earned her first paycheck. The first time she tried to deposit her check into Frank's account, she was told she could not do so because her name was not on the account.

"I don't understand; this is my husband's account. Don't I have access to it as well?" Diane questioned.

"Not exactly, ma'am. You are listed as a beneficiary, which means you are entitled to the money in the event of the account holder's death. The account holder would have to add your name to the account, which would allow you to make deposits, withdrawals, and any other changes." The teller explained.

Diane cashed the check instead. By the second time she went to the bank to cash her check, a teller suggested something that caught her attention, "May I interest you in opening an account with us, madam?" This transition to independence and being the breadwinner of her household was all happening so fast she never even considered getting her own account. Although juggling her job, visiting Frank in the hospital and spending time with Lori could get overwhelming, leaving the bank with an account in her name made Diane feel powerful, and it gave her a sense of self-reliance.

Diane came home that day in a cheerful mood, "Lori, do you want to go into town with me? Maybe get some ice cream?"

Lori gladly tagged along. Downtown Chicago in Spring was a sight to see; the streets were busy but not hectically overcrowded, and even the tallest man felt like an ant surrounded by high-rises that soared more than fifty stories into the sky. The stench of sauerkraut swayed in the wind as hot-dog stands were posted on the corners of busy boulevards. Diane and Lori stopped at Coleman's Creamery, a popular ice cream parlor. The ladies made small talk over double-scoop vanilla ice cream cones while strolling through a nearby riverfront park.

Diane suggested, "How about a ferry ride across the bay?"

"You're just full of surprises today, aren't you?" Lori said, pleasantly surprised at her mother's spontaneity.

"So, how's school?" Diane asked as the wind flailed her hair around.

Lori responded as she slurped on her ice-cream cone, "School is good, nothing new. How's work?" It still felt weird being able to ask her mother that.

"Work is good. I'm still getting used to the atmosphere, but the boss is kind of an asshole."

"Mom!" Lori exclaimed, nearly choking on her ice cream.

"What? It's true." Diane giggled with a shrug. Diane did not appreciate Lou's behavior; he demanded things, he was rude, and he never let a lady pass by without pinching her bottom.

"I don't ever want to hear you say that word again." Lori laughed. For a second, she almost forgot she was with her mom; they were actually laughing together and having a good time. Perhaps without Frank's stern presence constantly hovering over them, Lori and Diane could finally be themselves around each other.

"So, mom, what did you want to do with your life before you met dad?"

"Honey, I grew up in the 40s. You know women didn't have many options back then." She sighed in between her remark. "However, as a young girl, I dreamed of being in the first professional women's baseball league."

"Really?" Lori could not believe what she was hearing.

"Yes. They were called *The All-American Girls Professional Baseball League.* When they hit the scene, they caught the attention of the entire country; it was a great distraction from all the devastation surrounding the war." Diane told Lori all about the *All-American Girls* and how popular they were; always being mentioned in the newspaper and on the radio. Lori was surprised to hear this untold story and tried to imagine her mother on a baseball field, pitching, catching, and scoring homeruns.

"Wow, I wasn't expecting you to say that."

"I know, but my baseball dreams would have been short-lived anyways because I was terrible at baseball. I could never even get a hit. Let's just say I wasn't *All-American Girls* material." Diane laughed, nearly slumping over in her seat as Lori chuckled along with her. "The thing I've always been good at was writing."

"I never knew that." Lori wondered why this was her first time finding out these things about her mom. Diane told Lori about her own mother having a brief career as an English teacher during World War II, which was how Diane got interested in writing in the first place.

Diane spoke about the empowerment she felt upon seeing her mother provide for the household during that time. "There was something special about seeing my mother work and support her family; it made me feel like a woman could do anything."

Diane went on to detail how she was eight when the war started for the United States, and that the men were away for several years, leaving the workforce to be provisionally taken over by women. Diane concluded the story with, "My dad returned home from the war in 1945, and my mom quit her job as a teacher to resume her life as a housewife", ending their delightful conversation on a slightly less cheerful note.

Suncoast Ventures was in the business of life insurance: billing customers, collecting monthly premiums, processing claims and paying out policies. As the weeks rolled by, Diane was becoming more confident in her abilities and more comfortable in her work environment.

"Could someone get me a cup of Joe?" Lou hollered while chomping on a jelly-filled donut. Diane took the initiative and did so. As she carefully set the cup of hot coffee down on his desk, Lou placed his heavy hand on her backside and rubbed it slightly, "Thanks, Sweet Cheeks."

Diane's eyes narrowed, and she *accidentally* spilled scorching hot coffee all over Lou. The scalding liquid burned his lap and crotch. Lou howled in pain like a coyote.

"Whoopsie! Clumsy me." Diane yelped in an exaggerated tone.

Lou waddled away in pain to the nearest restroom to address his wounds. The other female employees noticed the incident and giggled; some even muttered under their breath, "Serves him right" and "She got him good."

After work, Diane and Lori went by the hospital to see Frank.

"Hello dear, how are you feeling?" Diane asked as she greeted Frank with a kiss on his cheek.

"I'm feeling better; I should be out of here in a few more weeks," Frank explained. "How is everything with you ladies?" He asked while skimming through a few unread sections of the morning paper.

"School is good, I have a B average, and there's a dance this Friday night. Everyone is going." Lori answered enthusiastically.

"That's great doll, have fun. And you, Diane?"

"Work is going well, all of our past due bills are paid, and I opened a checking account recently."

"You did what? Why did you open a new account?"

"I had no other choice, dear; my name isn't on any of your accounts, remember?" Diane responded in a snide manner, which wasn't like her.

"Watch your tone, Diane," Frank warned her not to provoke his anger.

Diane chose her next words carefully. "The banker simply suggested I open my own account rather than cash my checks each week. It just isn't safe for a woman to be walking around with that kind of money."

Frank went along with it for the time being.

The following day, Lori sat in geometry class and watched as her teacher jotted away on the blackboard with a fresh piece of chalk. Drew locked eyes with Lori's and began mouthing something to her, but she could not fully make out what he was saying. He resorted to scribbling something on a piece of paper and passing her a note instead.

He wrote: *Big dance Friday night. Have a date?*

She wrote: *Not yet. Why?*

Drew responded: *Was thinking you + me?*

Lori turned her head and gave him a smile of approval. She doodled in her notebook and wondered what her classmates would say when she and Drew show up at the dance together like Cinderella and Prince Charming.

After school, Lori headed to her parents' bedroom. The benefit of having the same shoe size as her mom was being able to raid her closet for cute heels. As she rummaged through her mother's closet, looking for shoes to wear to the dance, she found a couple of old journals and a folder filled with sheets of loose paper covered in writing.

Lori skimmed the articles and found delightful poems and whimsical short stories written by her mother. It was clear to Lori that her mother was talented. She took the folder to her room and fell into the tellings of a young Diane. Romance, comedy, and suspense were among the different themes Diane's writing focused on. The interesting adventures and amusing anecdotes kept Lori occupied for hours. A few days later, Lori had finally finished reading her mother's material.

"Mom, these are great!" Lori raved with the old journal in her hand.

"I forgot about these. Where did you find them?" Diane said as she flipped through the ancient pages.

"Buried in a shoebox, deep in your closet. I remember you saying you liked to write when you were younger, but these really blew me away." Lori doted over her mother's writing. "Mom, I think you should be a writer."

"It's not that simple, Lori."

"At least consider this," Lori said while taking a classified page ripped from a newspaper with a section circled.

Diane took the piece of paper from Lori and read it aloud. "Open position at the Chicago Tribune. Looking for a journalist. The salary is $3.00 an hour! If you qualify, apply at our office downtown."

Diane felt little butterflies fluttering around in her stomach; maybe this could be the first step toward her going after what she wanted. Seeing that typewriter at her job and retrieving her old story folder from Lori, re-awakened something in Diane she thought she had lost. She spent the whole night in her bedroom with a pen and notebook and filled over ten pages with new content. This time around, her writing style was passionate, thoughtful, and more mature overall. Diane was impressed by her own work and made a mental note to apply to the *Chicago Tribune.* With any luck, Frank might have a change of heart about her working by then.

Saturday morning, Diane noticed Lori on the phone with one of her school chums, chattering about the dance last night. Lori went on and on about Drew, who had "the most beautiful eyes." She explained how closely he held her when they danced and how she wished the night would not end. It was funny; looking at Lori was like going back in time and looking at herself. She did not mean to eavesdrop, but she heard so much of herself at that age in her daughter's voice. Diane quit being nosy and prepared to do a load of laundry.

That night, there was an unusual silence coming from Lori. Normally, she would be clamoring about her day by now. Diane noticed Lori's demeanor and uttered, "Something on your mind, honey. You seem distracted?"

"Actually, yes. I have a question to ask you. Are things going to change when dad comes back home?"

Diane questioned, "Change in what way?"

"I just mean, it's been kind of nice around here lately. Just the two of us."

"Oh, sweetie, aren't you excited your father is coming home?"

"I am. I mean, I was just getting used to you being a working woman."

"Lori, me working was only supposed to be a temporary thing until your father got back on his feet. He'll be home soon, and things will go back to normal." Even as the words came out of her mouth, Diane questioned if she was ready to rescind back into her mundane role as a stay-at-home mom.

Easter Sunday fell on April 6th this year, and Diane used some extra money to buy herself a new outfit for church. She made an appearance sporting a new knee-length skirt with a matching top, a pearl necklace, white gloves, and a pillbox hat. For the most part, Diane's wardrobe was more relaxed, but today, she dressed to impress. Diane and Lori spent a few hours visiting Frank after church. Frank had been making major strides in his physical therapy and was scheduled to be released in just a couple of days. "Diane, bring my briefcase from the office, will you? I need to finish up some reports before the deadline. One of the maintenance workers will leave my office unlocked for you." Frank ordered, and Diane nodded in compliance.

The next afternoon, Diane headed over to Frank's workplace to retrieve his briefcase. She took the day off so she would have more than enough time to fetch Frank's belongings and get the house in order for his return the next day. She walked into the small office and opened the first drawer filled with old paperwork, pens, and menus from nearby eateries. She opened the next drawer and immediately found the briefcase, but there was something shiny peeking through the paperwork; it was a small, metal key just about the size of the keyhole on that lockbox she found in her basement. "This must be it," she thought to herself. She shoved the tiny key in her purse and grabbed the briefcase before heading back to the hospital.

Later on, Diane arrived home, practically foaming at the mouth. This was too perfect; she almost didn't want to open the box for fear of whatever might happen next. She exhaled deeply and inserted the key with caution.

Once the box was opened, Diane discovered a couple of receipts. One was from a florist for flower arrangements and the other receipt was from a local lingerie boutique. This was strange because She did not remember receiving these items from Frank. She also noticed a Wisconsin postcard made out to Frank just weeks before his accident, but it was forwarded to his work address. It read:

My Dearest Frank,

I am missing your eyes, your smile, and your touch. I dream about when we will see each other again. We will make this Valentine's Day one to remember. Always thinking of you.

Forever Yours,

Sylvia

The woman did not leave a return address; she clearly did not want to leave a trail just in case her lover's wife ever became aware of his infidelities, but that moment was happening now.

Diane didn't even bother tracking the other woman down and threatening her to leave her Frank alone; she was emotionally exhausted. Every so often, the phone would ring, and when Diane answered, the person would hang up. She did not read too much into it at the time, thinking it was probably just some rascals prank calling. But perhaps it was this Sylvia woman the whole time, waiting to hear Frank's voice on the other line but ending the call when she heard the feminine tone of his spouse instead.

"Lori, have you noticed anything unusual going on around here lately?"

"What do you mean?" Lori asked.

"Like strange phone calls or pieces of mail; like letters or postcards."

"No, not really. There was one thing that happened, but that was months ago, just before dad's accident."

"What happened?" Diane asked, now interested.

"It was early one morning, and I caught dad on the phone; he was whispering, but I just thought he didn't want to wake us. When dad saw me, he was acting kind of weird and secretive, like he didn't want me to hear who he was talking to." Lori explained. "Why? Is everything okay?"

"Of course, sweetie." Diane lied and sealed it with a smile; there was no need to involve Lori in these adult matters. That phone call must have been between Frank and Sylvia. She wrote him a love note just weeks before he left for Milwaukee, Wisconsin, and he was probably calling to confirm their romantic rendezvous. Sylvia must have been the real reason behind his many "business trips" over the years.

Diane's mind was all over the place. She tried to recollect the past few years and asked herself how she could have missed the signs of her husband cheating all along. This ordeal was a bit much for Diane to wrap her head around.

Diane felt disgusted; this was not the life she wanted for herself, to be married to a controlling, pompous, serial cheater. Diane was only 19 when she married her much older and experienced, 25-year-old suitor, Frank. He came from a good family, and Diane's parents wanted to see her marry well to secure her future. Over the years, Frank had groomed Diane into the woman he wanted her to be—she was obedient, even-tempered, and not too friendly or talkative, especially around other men. Yet here Frank was, carrying on an affair with another woman! Shaken with frustration, Diane did not know how she would be able to face Frank again—and the worst part was that he was coming home tomorrow.

Chapter 3

Through The Grapevine

The next morning, Frank was eager to finally leave the hospital. It had been two months since the accident, and Frank had completed all his physical therapy sessions. He received the official green light from his doctor to be discharged and resume work.

He observed his wife as she came to pick him up from the front entrance of the hospital. So much about Diane had changed; she had better posture, and she projected her voice when speaking. This new confidence was practically radiating off her. Lori was proud of her mother's metamorphosis, but she feared that Frank still had the ability to pound Diane back into her former submissive self.

The whole car ride home, Frank yammered on and on about how happy he was to be released from the hospital. Diane's body was present, but her mind was elsewhere. She hid her apprehension behind a smile and helped Frank with his bags as he entered his estranged home. Diane washed her hands and tied an apron around her waist to get dinner started. She opened the harvest yellow refrigerator door and tried to remember the ingredients she needed to prepare the meal. To her displeasure, the only thing she could think about was that postcard and the woman who wrote it. Diane struggled to stay focused as her mind was invaded by intrusive thoughts. Diane wondered what this woman looked like; was she younger than her? Better looking? More adventurous in bed?

Diane held her tongue for as long as she could until the question finally seeped from her mouth, "Who is Sylvia?" she asked.

"What?" Frank replied, as if he did not hear the question the first time.

"Sylvia! Who is Sylvia, Frank?" Diane repeated.

"I don't know what the hell you're talking about." Frank said, too much of a narcissist to admit his mistakes.

"Really? Because I found this hidden in our basement!" Diane exclaimed as she presented her findings from the day before.

Frank examined the familiar postcard and changed the subject. "Were you going through my stuff?"

"No, I found the key to your little secret box when I stopped by the office to get your briefcase." Diane clarified. "So, who is she?"

"Diane, I have been cooped up in a hospital bed for the past 2 months! I was expecting to come home to a hot meal and a warm bath, not one of your crazy tangents."

"Trust me, I was in a much better mood before I found this love note from your mistress." Diane retorted, uncharacteristically having a response to every one of Frank's statements.

Frank pointed out, "Keep your voice down. Lori is in the other room."

Diane scoffed, unfazed that Lori might hear their argument, secretly hoping Lori would find out what kind of man her father really was so Diane would not feel so alone in her state of disappointment. "I can't do this. I'm going to stay at Betty's for a while."

Frank was not sure if he heard correctly, or if he was just hallucinating from the medication, but the fierceness in Diane's eyes was all the reassurance he needed. "Have you lost your mind?" Frank said as he tightly grabbed her by the arm. "No wife of mine is going to stay over that big-mouth Betty Morris's house."

"Call me when you're ready to explain yourself," Diane said as she shook Frank's grip off her.

At that moment, Diane was almost unrecognizable, her demeanor shifted drastically; she held her head up high and no longer cowered in fear of Frank's presence. She aggressively packed a few bags and walked out the front door.

Diane ended up on Betty's front porch, crying and upset. Betty let her in and grabbed her bags while asking what was wrong. Diane sat on Betty's sofa and poured her heart out.

"Apparently, Frank has been seeing some floozy in Wisconsin named Sylvia. He bought her flowers and lingerie for Valentine's Day; I saw the receipts. He has a hard enough time remembering our anniversary, and here he is planning romantic weekends with some tramp who lives almost two-hundred miles away," she described while tears streamed down her face.

"That man is a real bastard. Honestly, Diane, what are you holding on to?" Betty asked while offering Diane a Kleenex.

Diane blew her nose into the tissue and found herself at a roadblock to answer Betty's question. What was she sticking around for? Bad communication and a mediocre sex-life? Truthfully, it was the social pressure to stay married, fear of admitting to herself that her marriage had failed and not wanting to disappoint her daughter that was keeping Diane committed to Frank for all these years.

One day, someone called for Diane, and Lori took a message. She brought a piece of paper with the stranger's name and number to Betty's house and gave it to her mother. Diane read the information and called the person back. The phone rang until someone finally answered.

"Hello." The stranger said.

"Good afternoon, this is Diane Sutton. I am returning a call from this number."

"Hello, Diane. This is Charles Smith, editor-in-chief of the Chicago Tribune. Listen, we received your application about a month ago, and it was quite impressive. We would like to offer you a full-time position."

"Yes! Thank you so much!" Diane yelped with jubilance.

Mr. Smith provided instructions for Diane's first day.

Tears of joy nearly flowed from her eyes; she could hardly contain the happiness swelling up inside of her.

"What's with all the ruckus?" Betty asked.

"You are looking at The Chicago Tribune's newest journalist," Diane said as she pranced proudly through the foyer.

"What? Mom, that's amazing." Lori said before supportively embracing her mother.

"Way to go, Diane! Those people would be crazy not to hire you." Betty congratulated.

Later that day, Diane, Betty and Lori stopped by a local shopping mall. When the neighbors started noticing that Diane would leave for work from Betty's house and not her own, they began cultivating rumors. She found herself morally conflicted, wondering if this temporary separation was just a gateway to her walking away from her marriage. She could hear the not-so-subtle whispers while others pointed as she walked by. Fully aware that the neighborhood was a cesspool of gossip and drama, she ignored the speculations, and then she suddenly ran into none other than Barbara Ross.

"Hello Diane, Betty. I hear you two are living together now." Barbara said in a rude tone.

"Frank and I have been having some problems lately. I've been staying with Betty so I can clear my head." Diane explained in an effort to set the record straight.

"So, you'd rather shack up with another woman than be home with your own husband? Well, I suppose the rumors were true." Barbara said under her breath, insinuating some kind of girl-on-girl romance between them.

Betty rolled her eyes and bellowed, "Barbara, why don't you mind your own business for once?"

"Hey, I'm not here to judge your situation, but Betty, you should be ashamed of yourself for even encouraging this kind of behavior! You won't be satisfied until Diane is single and bitter like you. If you were a real friend, you would talk some sense into Diane and tell her to go back to her husband." Barbara masked her nosiness with concern.

"Diane is doing what's best for her. Just Stay out of it." Betty advised.

Barbara pulled Diane to the side and said, "I don't know what's going on between you and Frank, but whatever he did, just forgive him. People are starting to talk. I mean, you don't really want to end up like Betty, do you? Just look at her, overweight and unmarried; she's hopeless." Brainwashed by the narrative that it was better for a woman to be married and miserable than a thirty-something year old divorcee, Barbara offered a pitiful display of what she thought was helpful advice.

"I'd better get going," Diane said, excusing herself from the unwanted conversation. She was still so overjoyed by the serendipitous phone call from earlier, not even Barbara could ruin her good mood.

Traffic rushed through the streets; the sounds of engines revving and cars honking filled the air. Diane's feet buckled in her high heels, as she stood in front of a towering high-rise building downtown, where the Chicago Tribune was located up on the 20th floor. According to her watch, if she did not get in there soon, she would be late for her first day. Diane swallowed her inhibitions and stepped into the colossal structure, barely ready to conquer this next chapter of her life.

She stepped into the establishment and was stunned by the hustle and bustle of the newspaper editorial. The office was broken up into sections, and journalists covered stories as they clicked and clacked away on typewriters. The stories then went through the process of being proofread, edited and formatted before finally being published in the paper. The illustrators drew the comics in the Sunday papers, swiveling around in rolling chairs.

Diane was introduced to another journalist by Mr. Smith. "Diane, meet Bruce Walters; he is our senior journalist and one of the best writers we have on the team. He'll show you the ropes. If you have any questions, don't be afraid to ask."

When Bruce stood up, he loomed over her with a pen tucked behind his ear. Diane was flustered by his smile as he gently took her hand and greeted her with a firm handshake.

"Good to meet you," he said warmly.

Charles gathered everyone around and made a brief announcement as he presented Diane to the rest of the team. "Everyone, I would like to introduce you all to Diane Sutton; she is our newest journalist. Diane, we are excited to have you join our team. We make it a priority to let our staff know that our female employees are just as important as our male employees. Let's all just show respect to one another." Diane was once again the new girl but in a completely different setting this time around. She could feel how much more inviting and professional this work environment was than her last.

Over the next few weeks, Diane was in training. Bruce got her better acquainted with the department staff and familiar with the company's practices and policies. Bruce was very knowledgeable about the trade and open to answering any questions she may have had.

"The first story Charles wants you to cover is the formation of the Rainbow Coalition, founded by Fred Hampton, a Chicago native and member of the Black Panther Political Party," Bruce explained.

"The Black Panther Party? Is that safe?" Diane asked, worried after seeing several of Frank's favorite news outlets paint the Black Panthers in a negative light.

"That's going to be for you to judge. We have footage of the founder and his followers talking about the organization and its purpose. After observing and analyzing the information, you will have everything you need to start writing your piece on what you've researched." Bruce detailed the process.

"Get to work because the Rainbow Coalition is going to be opening a daycare center in the South side of Chicago next week, and I want you there taking notes." Charles made his prospects very clear and expected Diane to deliver; he knew she was more than capable of putting together a great story.

Diane watched footage of the press documenting Fred Hampton along with leaders from different racial backgrounds gathering and signing documents, officiating the formation of the Rainbow Coalition. Fred shook hands with his allies and smiled for the cameras as bigots resentfully scowled at this display of different races banding together and uniting for equality.

Sunday morning, as Lori got dressed for church, she was still uneasy about the current living arrangement between her parents. She brushed her hair in front of the mirror and hoped that today's service would put her in better spirits. Lori invited Drew to accompany her and Diane. The trio sat in the pew of the front row, ready to hear the good word that Sunday morning. After the service, Pastor Wright spotted Diane and the kids and came over to give his salutations.

"Praise God! Look at the beautiful young people. It warms my heart to see today's youth make time to visit the house of the Lord." He said energetically. Diane smiled at his remark as she always made sure to expose Lori to the church during her upbringing. "Good morning, pastor. It's good to see you. This is Lori's friend Andrew." Diane spoke.

"Yes, I remember Drew from the neighborhood. Things between you two sure are getting serious. Do I hear wedding bells?" Pastor Wright teased.

"Pastor, leave that child alone. She's too young to be thinking about marriage," Diane said, quickly shutting down the thought of Lori walking down the aisle anytime soon.

"I'm just saying, I think it's cute. Lori and Drew remind me of you and Frank when you both were younger."

That comment nearly made Lori shudder. Ending up in a loveless marriage like her parents was Lori's worst nightmare. She tried to hide her disdain at his comment.

Meanwhile, home did not quite feel the same without the warm and comforting element Diane and Lori brought to it. Frank was beginning to feel the effects of this separation. Food was not being cooked, dishes were not getting done, and laundry was not getting washed. Filth was piling up in the house. Lori pitched in and assumed the household chores to help keep the clutter at bay. Too stubborn to learn how to work the appliances, Frank was running out of fresh clothes to wear; he felt such tasks were beneath him. He spent many of his days all alone in an empty house.

Frank was also drinking more often now to cope with the loneliness. He found nightly solace in a glass of cognac filled to the rim with liquid poison; he drank until the things that bothered him didn't bother him anymore.

Sunday evening, Drew picked up Lori and took her for a drive before parking on a hill with a great view of the modest town below. They exited the vehicle, and Lori sat in the backside of the shag-carpeted van as Drew stood and looked over the skyline. Lori shivered slightly from the chilly night air, and Drew covered her with his leather jacket. They could see the whole town from this spot. In clear view, the fluorescent lights from Milo's dinner, where they had their first date, flickered slightly. The pair held hands in awe that it had already been a year since they met.

Drew reached into his pocket and said, "I love you, Lori," before presenting her with a shiny promise ring. "I was hoping we could go steady." Lori's expression, however, was not what he expected. Drew stood there, confused because Lori was not showing more gratitude for his amorous gesture.

"What's wrong? Don't you like it?" He stammered.

"I think it's beautiful, but what does this mean?"

"It means…I want us to commit to being together. I want you to wear my promise ring."

Lori was so intimidated by the words, "promise" and "commit," she could not even return the "I love you" or appreciate his sweet words. Drew's actions seemed like a mini marriage proposal, and Lori was not ready for it.

She tried to let him down gently, "I'm sorry Drew, but I think we should slow down, we're too young to be committing anything to each other."

Lori's paranoia had fast-forwarded her mind to her being hitched, barefoot and pregnant all before the age of 21, just like her mother. Tension began to build up in the van, so Drew decided to take Lori home as that evening came to an unpleasant end.

The next day at school, Lori was hanging out by the lockers with her classmate, Vanessa. Drew made his way through the halls, avoiding eye contact with Lori. "Drew, I hope you're not still mad about last night," Lori stopped him and reached for a hug, but he brushed her off and headed to class.

"Ouch." Vanessa reacted to the cold shoulder Lori just received. "Trouble in paradise?" She asked.

"He gave me a promise ring last night," Lori explained.

"Really? Let me see it," Vanessa said, eager to look at the trinket.

"I didn't take it. Everything between us is just moving so fast—I told him we needed to take a break."

"You turned down free jewelry? You really need to sort out your priorities," Vanessa said, while checking her reflection in a compact mirror.

During class, sitting next to Lori was nothing short of torture for Drew. With a perfect view of the girl who broke his heart, he had to sit there and act unaffected by her troublesome words from the night before. With a pad on his desk, Drew acted as if he was taking notes. Remembering Lori's words made him tense up, and his fingers applied so much pressure on the pencil in his hand, he thought he would break it. The teacher noticed Drew's disposition and asked if he was okay. Drew stormed out of the classroom and into the hall before ditching class completely.

During supper, Diane noticed Lori only took a few bites from her favorite meal and asked, "Everything okay, sweetie? You hardly touched your food."

"Yeah, I'm fine, just not hungry." Lori insisted, but her body language suggested otherwise as she slumped in her chair with her elbow on the dining table.

"Are you sure? You look a little down." Diane asked, pointing out the obvious.

"That's because Drew and I broke up," Lori revealed.

"Why honey?"

"Things were just moving so fast. He gave me a promise ring, but I didn't accept it. I don't want to make a promise I can't keep."

"As long as you were honest with him and yourself, you have nothing to feel guilty about."

The following day, Diane was sent on her first assignment to cover the grand opening of a daycare center, run by Fred Hampton and fellow black panther members. Arriving in the south side of Chicago was like stepping into an alternate universe, where most communities were stricken with poverty. Public housing developments were on every corner and those disadvantaged areas were a stomping ground for poverty, crime, and harassment against Black citizens by hostile police officers.

Diane brought only a pen, notepad, and a polaroid camera with her to the grand opening. She entered the child-care center and observed mostly black employees serving cereal and milk to the children of the disadvantaged members of that community.

"Mr. Hampton, some say that his daycare operation is just a coverup for some kind of illegal activity. What do you have to say about that?" A member of the press asked.

"Mister, as you can see, we are running a daycare and providing safe and affordable childcare for the low-income families in this neighborhood. That's all we're trying to do; we don't want any problems."

Diane was enthralled by this eye-opening display of humanity; she stood on the sidelines and observed a group of people giving back and helping uplift each other during a time of crisis. Diane had never witnessed such acts of kindness before. Watching that gesture and the magnitude of effects it had on their community warmed her heart. It made her wonder how difficult life must have been for Black people and the types of hardships they faced. Those people on the South side were forgotten and no one seemed to be helping, so they had to help each other. Diane gathered all the information she needed and wrote a compelling expose on the prolific civil rights activist.

In all, the Rainbow Coalition stands for equality for all humankind, they believe that no one should be considered inferior to others or be denied basic privileges due to their race, gender, ethnicity, or economic status. In an effort to combat the obstacles that systemic oppression has placed before them, the Rainbow Coalition unites to fight social injustices in Chicago and throughout the United States.

The writing staff applauded as Diane read the conclusion to her article aloud, and Charles complimented her on a job well done. Diane gladly accepted their praises and thanked her accomplishment to Bruce's guidance. She acknowledged his patience and persistent willingness to help. Bruce was very socially aware and showed compassion towards victims of racial, religious, and sexist injustices. Conversations with Bruce opened up the floodgates to a whirlwind of information on what was happening throughout the United States and the rest of the world. Bruce had a fascination with history and human behavior. In college, he had muddled through complex theories on why people acted the ways that they did.

It had been nearly a month since Diane had been staying at Betty's, and Frank expected her to be back by now. Frank finally came to his senses and insisted on having a conversation with Diane to see if they could work things out. In true Frank fashion, he didn't necessarily apologize for his actions, but more so for the actions of the other woman. He assured Diane that his relationship with Sylvia was nothing more than a meaningless fling, but Sylvia had gotten a little too attached. Frank explained that he had met Sylvia years ago and that she had practically thrown herself at him.

"You know how competitive you women are. A single lady sees a happily married man and makes it her mission to sleep with him, simply because she wants what she can't have."

Diane wondered if Frank would utter the same words if Sylvia were right there in the room. Frank's statement left things open-ended and did not answer relevant questions like, if this was just a fling, why was Frank hiding keepsakes in the basement? Nevertheless, Diane was slightly influenced by Barbara's comments from the last time they spoke and agreed to put Frank's indiscretion behind her so that they could move on.

"Great, now that this is settled and you're coming back home, you can put in your two-week notice at your job."

"Actually, Frank, I—"

"Mom, you're quitting?" Lori asked. "But you love your job."

"Don't be silly, Lori. Of course she's quitting." Frank answered on Diane's behalf before sending Lori to her room.

"Frank, I really think we should talk about this—" Diane's comment was once again interrupted by Frank's remark.

"There's nothing to talk about, Diane. I need you home, end of story. Also, you can go ahead and close that bank account you opened. You won't be needing it any longer."

Diane's blood pressure rose from frustration. First, finding out about Sylvia, then Frank barking orders and having the nerve to expect Diane to surrender the things she had worked so hard for. She finally had enough and sternly said, "No!"

"Excuse me?" When Frank barged back into his home, his mission was to reassert himself as the alpha male of the household, but that plan was derailed by Diane's internal growth.

"You heard me. I'm not closing my account and I'm not quitting my job. I used to spend all day cleaning your house, driving your cars, and using your money. This is mine and I'm not giving it up."

Of course, Frank's pride would never allow him to let a woman speak to him in such a way. He replied, "How dare you speak to me like that! I am your husband. Now you listen to me, Diane, I am the man; I pay the bills, I make the rules."

Frank rampaged through the kitchen, screaming so loud that little globs of saliva flew out of his mouth. The vein in his head throbbed, and he even knocked a glass off the counter, sending it smashing into a million pieces. This sparked an argument between them.

"This is exactly why I didn't want you working. Now you have this notion in your mind that you call the shots, and I won't stand for it."

Diane replied, "Of course not! Someone with an ego as fragile as yours couldn't possibly tolerate a woman who speaks up for herself. You just need someone to control because you're desperate to validate your manhood, and it's pathetic."

"What did you just say?" Frank's yells carried on throughout the spacious home, the aggression in his voice made the environment so uncomfortable that Lori could no longer stay seated. Lori crept over to the edge of the dining room wall to get a look at the altercation, and what happened next was something she was not prepared to witness. Frank sent Diane flying up against the kitchen countertop after smacking her across the face. The blood from her lip painted the backside of Frank's large hand. Diane spat the blood from inside her mouth onto Frank's face.

Lori became hysterical, pounding on her father's back, screaming, crying, and begging him to stop assaulting her mother. Lori knew of Frank hitting her mother in the past, but she had never witnessed any of the beatings herself. She would see Diane occasionally cover bruises with makeup here and there, but it was not a common occurrence. It was hard for Lori to stay neutral as she stood there and watched her father flagrantly mistreat her mother.

Diane's head was spinning from the series of events that had led her to this exact moment. Perhaps it was the physical abuse, or Frank's infidelities and his controlling ways that finally pushed her over the edge. Diane went into a frenzy; she could no longer control herself. Rationality was no longer present, and her emotions became truth. She gathered a few of Frank's most prized possessions and placed the items on the grill in the backyard. She poured lighter fluid on his golden Rolex watch, his Fiorucci jacket, and a vial of expensive cologne before setting them ablaze. Diane's fury flared out of control like the fire she ignited, and she was a blazing inferno, unleashing her wrath like only a scorned woman could. She was furious and unable to make eye contact with Frank without feeling overwhelmed with anguish.

Lori followed her mother outside to check on her and hollered when she caught a glimpse of Diane in the backyard. "Mom, what are you doing? Please stop!"

This was not a momentary lapse in judgment; this was years of built-up frustration finally boiling over. The neighbors stood around and made a spectacle of the commotion. They gasped and covered their mouths in disbelief. It was not long before the police showed up. The authorities received a call from one of the neighbors about a disturbance in the area. Diane's wrists were bound by metal handcuffs before she was led to the back of the patrol car. Lori cried profusely and groveled, her knees nearly touching the ground, begging the officers not to arrest Diane.

"Dad, don't let them take her! Do something!"

Frank scanned the faces of all the bystanders and quietly entered the home, mortified. Diane turned slightly in the back seat and stared out the rear windshield as the police car drove off.

Chapter 4

Devil's Advocate

The police officers arrived at Shady Palms Mental Hospital, an insane asylum on the other side of town, and escorted Diane inside. "Not to worry, we'll take good care of her," the director said before ordering his staff to assign Diane to a room. She resisted as the staff dragged her through the halls. They brought her to a room and restrained her by strapping her onto a stretcher. One of the workers prepared a large needle and injected it into Diane's arm until she was fully sedated.

Meanwhile, Lori ran to Betty's house to let her know what had transpired. Betty and Lori rushed to the police department and were told that Diane had been transported to the psychiatric ward. Shortly after, they arrived at Shady Palms and went to the front desk to get more information on when Diane could be released.

"Her behavior was erratic when she was arrested, so we will need to conduct a psychiatric evaluation," the receptionist said.

"How long will that take?" Lori asked.

"At least 72 hours. If the evaluation determines she has a mental illness, she could be here longer," the receptionist said.

"Seventy-two hours? I'll be at my convention by then," Betty said, nearly forgetting that she had a work-related obligation in Springfield in just a few days. "Lori, go home and try to convince your dad to come back and get Diane out on Wednesday."

Diane woke up a few hours later. She felt her arms cross around her chest as she was bound by a straitjacket. The room was depressingly bleak, without a splash of color to liven it up. There was a full-sized metal bed with plain white sheets, white walls, and gray tile on the floor. Her first night at the asylum was ghastly; she cried most of the night.

Diane wondered if she had made the right decision, if working and establishing her independence was worth the havoc that had been wreaking havoc on her life lately. Shrouded by darkness, she was left all alone with only her thoughts to keep her company. She was forced to relive an incident she had buried in her memory years ago. This particularly painful memory occurred years ago when Diane was preparing for bed after a mild scuffle with Frank earlier that day. Frank crept up behind Diane as she sat before her vanity, rolling up her hair. He put his heavy hands on her shoulders, nearly weighing her down. He lowered her nightgown, exposing her back and asked, "Where is Lori?"

"She's at the drive-in with friends," she explained as she had just applied her last hair roller. Frank continued to caress her skin until she suddenly felt a sharp strike go across her back. She nearly fell to the floor from shock. The first lash to her spine caught her by surprise. When she turned around, she saw him wielding a leather belt. She attempted to get away, but he yanked her back and continued the assault.

Each lashing of the belt stung like alcohol on an open wound. Each welt-producing strike was harder than the last, making her screams rise an octave higher, hitting notes only an opera singer could reach. The force with which her husband whipped her sent an excruciating sensation down her body. The belt buckle broke her skin and left a stitch-worthy wound.

That action was the blueprint of their entire union. The last 17 years were condensed to a montage of thoughts that played in her mind; the revolving door of arguments and the toll Frank's overbearing control issues had taken on her over the years. She was a vessel, an empty shell of a woman when he was around. They had everyone fooled; friends and neighbors were under the impression that they were a normal and happy couple.

All the while, their sham of a marriage was the furthest thing from a happy relationship that Diane would not wish on her worst enemy. She was starting to doubt that she was ever in love with Frank, but she was fond of him in the beginning and hoped that they could grow old together. The only good thing that came from their marriage was Lori. She had spent several years tip-toeing around her husband, worrying about saying the wrong thing that could set him off. She believed that marriage was a sacrament, a bond meant to be positive, fruitful and protected by God—but there was nothing holy about this matrimony.

It had been nearly a full day since Diane arrived at the facility, and she still had not eaten. Her empty stomach sent her to the chow line. She eyed food service workers spooning questionable-looking grub onto metal trays. She took a seat and braced herself before shoving a spoonful of slop into her mouth. She felt so out of place, sharing the same space as women with undiagnosed mental illnesses labeled as "crazy". Shady Palms was also known to be a consequence for misbehaving wives. Several of the patients were sent by their abusive husbands for fighting back or displaying other troublesome behavior.

The next day after school, Lori was eating a snack in the dining room when she overheard Frank fraternizing with a few of his buddies from the neighborhood on the front porch.

"Hey there, Frank! How the hell are you? I heard you were in the hospital for a while," Pete Davis said. He was a notorious wife-beater in the community, originally from New Jersey. Unfortunately, everyone in the neighborhood took a passive approach to controversial issues; they did not intervene, they simply avoided the topic and then gossiped about it later.

"Yeah, I just came home. Then Diane starts bitching out of nowhere about some broad I got together with a few times," Frank said.

"Huh, women!" Pete scoffed.

"So, we get through that little situation. The next thing I know, she's spazzing out because I told her to quit her job. You know how that is; women start working, and they start feeling like they don't have to put up with their husband's crap. So, I smacked some sense into her," Frank added.

"That's how you gotta do it, Franky. When Marge starts getting on my nerves, I pop her right in the mouth, so she'll shut her trap," Pete laughed, with a cigar hanging out of his mouth.

"Diane ended up burning some of my stuff on the grill, and when the police showed up, they arrested her," Frank said.

"Yeah, that'll teach her," Pete laughed.

Lori made another attempt to get through to her father. "Dad, you have to do something! I'm worried about Mom," Lori pleaded, but she could not get through to him.

"It's for her own good," Frank insisted before going to bed.

Lori stood alone in the hallway, disgusted at how her father could sleep soundly while her mother was in a strange place, scared and alone.

71

Each day Diane and Lori talked on the phone; Diane would mention how aggressive the staff was with her for no apparent reason. After much begging and pleading, Lori finally managed to convince Frank to go see Diane. A couple of staff members led Diane to the visiting area of the facility and stood not too far behind. Her strange aloofness somehow made this encounter more uncomfortable than the last one. Diane had a glassy look in her eye as Frank sat across from her.

"Hello Diane. To be honest, I wasn't planning on coming to see you so soon, but Lori has been relentless," Frank admitted, thinking of all the places he'd rather be at that moment.

Diane sat in silence, still groggy from medication.

"I was hoping you had learned a valuable lesson on how a wife is to compose herself," Frank said.

Again, Diane provided no response.

"Are you ready, Diane? Ready to come back home? To play by my rules?" Frank berated her and basically threatened that if her attitude did not change, she would be stuck at Shady Palms indefinitely. Yet another manipulating intimidation strategy to force her into conformity. Diane's mind became distorted with anger, and she began to conceive violent thoughts. She fantasized about bashing his head repeatedly with a hammer until his skull cracked into a million pieces. She had to pull herself together; she was actually beginning to feel crazy. She continued to say nothing. In fact, she had so much to say that she did not know where to start and feared that if she started talking, she would have another meltdown. Frank grew tired of her muteness and informed Lori that she had five minutes to chat with Diane before he would head for the exit.

Lori noticed Frank looking down at his watch and tapping his foot impatiently, so she wrapped up her talk with Diane. "I love you, Mom. Stay strong," Lori left her mother with those simple words, knowing how desperately she needed to hear them. On the way out, Lori spotted her father chatting briefly with the director of the facility before shaking his hand. At that point, Lori feared something more sinister was at play, and she was right. In fact, Frank was secretly paying the director of the asylum to prolong Diane's stay and make it as uncomfortable as possible. This may have been Frank's most cruel tactic yet to keep Diane in line.

As more days passed, Lori felt she could no longer trust her father to get Diane out of Shady Palms. The facility kept using her "erratic behavior" as the excuse for withholding her. Betty was still out of town, and Lori was getting desperate for help since Frank was not very interested in rescuing Diane. Consequently, Lori took the city bus downtown and paid a visit to the Chicago Tribune in the hope that someone from her mother's job would be able to help.

Bruce was passing through the office with a stack of paperwork in his hands when he noticed a teenage girl wandering about. So, he asked, "Hello, young lady, is there something I can help you with?"

"Yes. Diane Sutton is my mother, and I need some help."

"Wait a minute, you're Diane's daughter? Where is your mom? She hasn't been to work in days. She's this close to getting fired," Bruce said, confused as to why Diane had been unreachable for nearly a week.

"My mom was sent to an asylum five days ago, and I'm not completely sure, but I think my dad is making them keep her for longer. Please, help me get her out."

Lori recounted all the events that led up to Diane's detainment at the mental facility and provided Bruce with the address of Shady Palms. Bruce wasted no time making his way to the clinic and entered the facility lobby. He demanded Diane be released immediately, but the receptionist hesitated after she looked at her clipboard and called the director down to the front desk.

The director appeared a few moments later and introduced himself with a friendly facade. "Good day, sir, how may I help you?"

"Hello, sir, my name is Bruce Walters, and I am here to collect Mrs. Diane Sutton. You can help me by preparing her discharge papers."

"I am sorry, but I will not be able to do that. The woman is mentally ill."

"Prove it. Show me her psychiatric evaluation." Bruce was not willing to accept such accusations without proof.

The director examined Bruce's hands and noticed he was not wearing a wedding band. "Are you, her husband?" The director asked rhetorically, as he already knew the answer to that question. "Then I'm afraid I won't be able to release that information to you, it would be against our policy. I find it quite unusual for a single man to take such an interest in a married woman."

"That's bullshit! You'll be hearing from my lawyer," Bruce stated before exiting.

The director did indeed get an unwelcome visit from Bruce's attorney the next day. The attorney claimed that the facility was wrongfully keeping a mentally stable person against their will and threatened to take the matter to court. The director followed up with a phone call to Frank.

"Listen up, Frank, I'm releasing your wife."

"What? Why would you do that? We had a deal!"

"I know that, but a gentleman came by yesterday morning, demanding Diane be released. He warned me that if she was not released, he would hire an attorney, Frank. I'm not going to jeopardize my business just so you can get back at your wife."

"A gentleman?" Frank asked, confused as to who could possibly be advocating for Diane.

The director went on to explain, "Yes, a younger fellow. He seemed to be in his early thirties, blonde hair, muscular build." Frank tried to maintain his composure before slamming the phone shut with rage.

Lori was elated when she discovered the news about Diane. She secretly called Bruce shortly after and they arranged to pick up Diane that same day. This mother/daughter reunion was an emotional one, as Lori practically jumped into Diane's arms and held onto her for what felt like forever when she appeared outside of the clinic.

Diane thanked Bruce profusely; she was so gracious that he would go through this much trouble to help her. Lori sat quietly in the backseat and watched her mother exchange intense looks with Bruce, who seemed to be more than just a friend from work. Diane stared at Bruce the way a damsel in distress might stare at her knight in shining armor when he came to rescue.

By the time the month of June rolled by, Diane had signed a lease and moved into her own apartment. She left the village of Huntley and found a place downtown, closer to her job. She rented a small but affordable two-bedroom unit on the fourth floor of an apartment building in a run-down neighborhood. She caught the bus to work each day, rain or shine, until she finally saved enough to buy a car—a 1963 Volvo 122S in good condition. The color was a pale yellow, and the interior was draped in stylish white leather. Work was also going well; Diane and Bruce were covering more stories and had grown even closer over the last couple of weeks. She thought that he had a brilliant mind and that he was truly ahead of his time. Bruce valued, appreciated, and respected women; those qualities made him even more appealing to her.

Diane found herself in a festive mood and decided to make the most out of her 800 square foot apartment by throwing a housewarming party. She invited Bruce, Drew, Pastor Wright and a few other people from the office to the celebration. Lori stormed over to her mother when she learned that Diane invited Drew in hopes that she would reconsider. Lori yapped about how things between her and Drew were still awkward and that she had been avoiding him.

"He's a nice boy, and just because you broke up doesn't mean you two can't still be friends," Diane said. "It's not going to kill you to be in the same room for a few hours. Now, help me set the table."

As the guests began to pour in with smiles and gifts in hand, Diane was grateful to have such supportive people in her life during this transition. She floated around the room while offering her guests hors d'oeuvres, on a crystal platter. She wore a red, knee-length halter dress that hugged her waist and flowed around with all of her movements.

When Bruce came through the door, Diane rushed over to greet him with a hug and took in the scent of his cologne. They got cozy in a corner tucked away from the rest of the festivities and conversed casually.

"Your party turned out great," he said with a cocktail in his hand.

"Thanks for coming, it means a lot." Diane had already divulged some details of her tumultuous relationship to Bruce so he knew how big of a step this was for her. Lori let Betty in and she joined them.

"Hello there." Betty said, excited to see Diane getting some male attention.

Diane introduced Betty to Bruce as they shook hands and exchanged salutations.

Drew dug into Diane's delicious appetizers and kept to himself most of the night. Lori was becoming increasingly uneasy; this was the last place she wanted to be—in a small apartment in between her ex, Drew and her mother's unofficial boyfriend. Diane locked eyes with Bruce and flirtatiously giggled every time he came in her vicinity. The chemistry between them was evident and Diane's undeniable interest in Bruce was sweet, but slightly uncomfortable for Lori. It was odd to see her mother interact with a man other than her father.

After the shindig, Betty stuck around to help clean up and was glued to Diane.

"Diane Elaine Sutton, I am impressed! Bruce is polite, easy on the eyes and he doesn't look a day over thirty." Betty said as she gushed over Bruce's facial features.

"He is 31, for your information", Diane clarified.

"Well isn't he a hot, young thing? You know what they say about younger men's libido. I hope you can keep up with that stud when the time comes." Betty suggested what Diane had only fantasized about.

It was needless to say that Diane was sexually frustrated; she and Frank had not slept together in months, and Bruce was looking better and better by the day. There was only so much satisfaction she could get from self-pleasuring. Her bed was cold and lonely nights would make her crave a warm, strong, manly body even more.

One stormy afternoon, as the rain poured, Diane turned up the radio slightly to better fill the room with "My Girl" by The Temptations. The antenna of the old, box-shaped radio was fully extended, and the music playing was occasionally interrupted by fluctuating static. A wave of bliss suddenly came over her. It was all starting to sink in, having a place to call home, and a moderately new car; these were the fruits of her labor. She was making the best of her situation, and she was just happy to be in her own space. She was happy enough to gyrate all over the small living room as the music played. She had not felt that happy in a long time.

Diane's joyful jig was interrupted by her mother, Eileen, barging in. "Mother?" Diane gasped, frightened by her unexpected visitor.

Slowly removing her shades, Eileen invited herself in and said, "Oh, dear God, it's worse than I thought." She took a better look around and grimaced at Diane's tiny apartment.

"Mother, what are you doing here? How did you even find out where I live?"

"I'll have you know that your husband called me, furious at your deplorable behavior! So, I looked you up in the phonebook and found you listed at this address," Eileen explained. Diane crossed her arms on the couch and turned her head in the opposite direction, ignoring her mother's yapping. "Okay, Diane, you've made your point. Now it's time to come home."

"I'm not going back. Frank hit me, in front of Lori!"

"Lori is a child; she doesn't understand the sacrifices women have to make to keep their families intact," Eileen explained, unconvinced that a slap across the face and a week at a psych ward were excuses for Diane to run out on her husband and dismantle her family. Eileen had had her fair share of bumps and bruises from the hands of her own husband, but Diane was ready to stop this generational curse in its tracks.

"Mother, don't be absurd. This has nothing to do with keeping the family together. This is about Frank desperately trying to convince himself that he still has control over me. Frank is awful; he's cruel and abusive."

"You know what your problem is? Ever since you started working, you're making your own money and you don't respect him anymore. Men need to provide; it makes them feel useful. It gives them purpose. If you take that away from him, what else does he have?"

"What are you talking about? You worked during your marriage," Diane pointed out.

"I didn't exactly have a choice, Diane; your father was away at war, so I did what had to be done to take care of my family. You're just being hard-headed," Eileen explained.

Lori had come home from school and could faintly hear her mother and grandmother's conversation from the other side of the front door. Lori listened for a while before coming in. Diane heard the doorknob jiggle and postponed the conversation for another time. "We'll discuss this later," Diane said.

"Hi, Grandma," Lori said, happy to see her.

"Hello, my sweet girl. It's been so long, how are you?" Lori and Eileen exchanged pleasantries and conversed for a few minutes while Diane stepped into the hall for a moment to get some air. She poked her head back into the apartment before re-entering.

"How are you coping with all of this foolishness between your parents?"

Lori, articulated, "I'm okay; things are still weird, but I'm adjusting."

"My goodness, this apartment is awfully small; you hardly have any space. Don't you miss your old room at your father's house?"

"I still go to my dad's every weekend and help him around the house, but Mom is happier here. I'd live in a supply closet if it meant seeing my mom happy." Lori had not noticed all the sacrifices her mother made to hold their family together over the years, but now she was ready to sacrifice comfort for her mother's happiness.

Eileen ended up spending a few more hours before she had officially worn out her welcome. "Well, I'm sorry you came all this way for nothing. Have a safe flight back home, Mother," Diane stated, as she rushed Eileen to the door before she could talk her into getting back with Frank.

"Whatever issues you and Frank have run into is nothing that can't be talked over," Eileen's efforts were relentless.

Diane felt as though she had reached her breaking point in this conversation. She and Eileen were talking in circles. It would have been nice to get some support from her mother, but it was clear to Diane that Eileen was not onboard with her decision to stay separated. Diane grew tired of explaining her reasons and began unbuttoning her blouse, exposing the black bra she had on underneath.

"Diane, what are you doing? Dear, please cover up," Eileen said, looking away. Diane proceeded to unhook the latch of her bra and turned around, exposing a significant scar on her back that had never fully healed. For years, Diane dared not to speak the disturbing truth about how violent Frank could be. Diane kept telling herself it could be worse, desperately trying to rationalize Frank's twisted behavior so she wouldn't have to accept the reality of the hell she was living.

Now she was showing off the scar to mother as a final attempt to convince Eileen not to interfere with her decision to leave Frank once and for all. Eileen shrieked in horror, her eyes began to tear up and her silence was an indication that she was finally listening to Diane's cry for help.

"Look at it, Mom! This is who I'm married to. What kind of person would do this to their wife? Is this the life you want for me?"

"Of course, not honey." Eileen said, trembling at the sight of how Frank had mutilated her child's body years ago. Eileen wept at the thought of Frank pushing Diane too far or hitting her too hard if he ever lost his temper and what the morbid outcome of that might be.

Eileen tried to compose herself but hearing her daughter's voice crack with agony made her break down as well. Diane exhaled with relief as she tapped into a deeper level of understanding with her mom. Eileen took her daughter by the hands and wiped the tears from her eyes like she did when Diane was a child and whispered, "You are stronger than I ever was."

Eileen secretly admired Diane for possessing the bravery she never had. Eileen wondered how different her life would have been if she had the strength to walk away from her own toxic marriage.

One evening, Diane made her way through the supermarket aisles, grabbing groceries from shelves and placing them in her cart. She was in the produce section when she noticed a sketchy-looking man lingering not far behind her. She glanced over her shoulder every now and then to see if the man was still there, and he was. She could feel the stranger staring at her; perhaps he was a criminal. The man wore all black and a baseball cap, so she couldn't get a good look at his face. She fearfully rushed to the checkout line and paid at the register. She sped out of the store and hastened the groceries into the trunk of her car. She could hear footsteps approaching. At that point, she wasn't sure if she was just being paranoid or if she was really being followed.

"Are you Diane Sutton?" the stranger asked.

"Yes, I am," Diane responded before instantly regretting it as the man reached for something in his coat. She was afraid the man had a knife or some other dangerous weapon. Diane was paralyzed with fear at the thought that Frank had found out about Bruce and paid someone to get rid of her for good. She considered making a run for it, but then she heard the stranger say, "You've been served." He handed her a large yellow envelope filled with divorce papers, making her feel silly for thinking someone was actually out to get her.

Back at the apartment, Diane curled up on the sofa with a bottle of red wine and the divorce papers spread out on the coffee table in front of her. Although she was strongly considering divorce, she never expected Frank to beat her to the punch. She took a pen from her purse to sign and initial the designated sections, inexplicably feeling hesitant about the papers that were spread out before her. Separating from her husband was one thing, but being faced with actual divorce papers was another; signing on the dotted line gave the end of their relationship such finality.

Chapter 5

Reap What You Sow

The second week of August, Bruce shared some thrilling news with Diane. "There's a huge festival happening in New York this weekend, and I need a co-editor. How would you like to cover the Woodstock Festival with me?"

"I would be honored," she stammered, surprised that Bruce trusted her with a story this provocative. With all the chaos surrounding the Vietnam War, Woodstock was intended to take a peaceful approach to bring people together and focus on their similarities rather than their differences.

"Great, our flight leaves in just a few days," Bruce smiled.

Working for the Chicago Tribune provided her with more than just a paycheck at the end of the week; it gave her social consciousness and self-awareness. She had lived a sheltered life and knew little of what was transpiring in the world around her. Human beings were getting blown away by the bombs dropping in Vietnam. President Nixon was determined to keep Americans divided, which perpetuated social crimes and injustices against minorities, especially African Americans. It was a frightful sight to see; it was as if humanity itself was crumbling. The atrocities people were committing against each other were truly staggering. Now, having knowledge of this left her feeling unsettled and hopeless. On the other hand, music seemed to be bringing people together more than ever. Recording artists like Bob Marley and the Beatles sang songs of togetherness, harmony, and love, inevitably influencing an entire community of people who would rather live peacefully than chaotically.

On Friday afternoon, Diane took a taxi to the airport. Giddy with excitement, her suitcase was packed the same night she found out about the assignment. After boarding the plane, Diane sat next to Bruce and her child-like enthusiasm was refreshing to him. She gazed out of the airplane window and repeated "oohs" and "ahhs" at the sight of the aircraft shredding through thick, fluffy clouds. She had never been on an airplane before. Three hours later, they arrived in the city of Bethel, New York, where the festival was being held. They landed around 7 p.m. that night and checked into a nearby hotel.

"You folks need a room?" the clerk asked.

"Two. Two rooms --- Two separate rooms." Diane over-clarified as she stuttered her statement.

Lately, everything involving Bruce felt like an erotic innuendo. Whether in was the way he licked his lips occasionally, suggestive eye contact or certain phrases he used during a conversation, it all made Diane feel the need to make it clear that there was nothing going on between them. Bruce grabbed the room keys, and they headed down the corridor to check out the rooms, which were right across the hall from each other.

Meanwhile, local teenagers were buzzing about some party at the University of Chicago that Saturday night. The party was for college kids to kick off the new school year, but a couple of high school students always tried to sneak in. This was turning out to be the worst summer ever; Lori and Drew were still avoiding each other, wasting away the perfect weather for bike riding in the park and swimming in the creek. Vanessa called Lori on the phone and asked if she wanted to go to the party.

"Hey, a bunch of us juniors are going to a party at the University of Chicago tomorrow night. You should come," Vanessa said.

"Yeah, I heard about it. I'm not really interested," Lori said.

On Saturday, August 16th, 1969, Bruce and Diane arrived early at the festival, first thing in the morning. They had missed the first day of the festival and had a lot to cover. Diane observed the audience arriving at the festival, who wasted no time sparking joints with lighters as they swayed their bodies left and right to the rhythm of the music playing. Hippies were viewed by conservatives as the underbelly of society; they were stigmatized as lazy, marijuana-smoking vagabonds who would not amount to anything. The crowd sang along in unison, and the performers' voices were engulfed by the chanting voices of the sea-like audience that stood before them.

Back in Chicago, Vanessa came by the apartment and made one last attempt to convince Lori to accompany her to the frat party that night.

"I told you, Vanessa, I'm not in the mood," Lori said, contemplating whether or not to go to the party while sulking over her breakup with Drew.

"Come on, Lori. You've been moping around since you split up with Drew. Let's have some fun," Vanessa said, poking her bottom lip out as she made a puppy dog face.

Vanessa's convincing visage persuaded Lori to agree. The girls got dressed and freshened up before taking the 20-minute drive to the university.

A huge party kicked off at the Gamma house, occupied by one of the most popular fraternities on campus. The frat brothers had their pledgers hoist in a keg and chug beer until they nearly collapsed from inebriation.

"Hey, glad you came!" said Nick, a popular student on a football scholarship

"Of course. We can't turn down a party," Vanessa said. "This is my friend Lori." Lori waved to the stranger, and he led the two young ladies to the living room.

"You girls want a beer?" he asked.

"Sure," Lori said enthusiastically, suddenly energized by the atmosphere.

After a few drinks, Vanessa saw some other classmates and joined them, eventually disappearing into the crowd. Since Vanessa was nowhere to be found, Nick kept Lori company in her absence. Drew happened to be at the same party. He sipped some dark liquor chased by cola as he strolled through the gathering and took in his surroundings. Stoners kept to themselves as they rolled up joints, while loose girls danced on tables in the living room. Lori relaxed on a sofa and knocked back a few beers with Nick. Between all the drama from her breakup with Drew and her parents' separation, Lori was longing for anything to make her feel better. Nick's company was turning out to be a great distraction from all the anxiety she was feeling. Drew tried not to notice as Nick whispered something in drunken Lori's ear that made her blush, but it was hard not to get jealous watching some guy sweet-talk his ex-girlfriend. Lori occasionally brushed away Nick's hands that wandered all over her body. She left his side to use the restroom. In her absence, Nick went into the kitchen to fix a couple more drinks.

When no one was looking, Nick dug into his shirt pocket and spiked Lori's drink with powder he emptied from a capsule. When Lori returned, he delivered the tampered beverage and listened to her throat gulp and glug as he waited for the drowse to set in. Fifteen minutes later, Lori could barely keep her eyes open; the barbiturate was working. As Drew danced from across the room, he noticed Nick helping Lori upstairs as she struggled to keep her balance. He guided her down the hall to an empty bedroom and locked the door behind him. She fell backward onto the bed, and Nick pulled her towards him as he lifted up her dress. Drew ran upstairs after them but was slowed down by intoxicated partygoers. As Lori laid on the bed, she could feel the warmth of his breath on her neck and the weight of his body on top of hers. She said faintly, "Nick, get off me." He ignored her and proceeded to remove her underwear.

Drew frantically searched the second floor of the frat house, bursting into random rooms only to find people having sex or doing drugs. He finally came across a locked door.

"Lori, are you in there?" he screamed. Lori tried to respond but could only make incoherent mumbles. Drew's patience was wearing thin, so he took a step back, raised his foot, and kicked the door in with all his might. The power from his blow broke the latch off the door and forced it open. Nick shivered from the shock of someone busting into the room.

"What the hell are you doing?" Drew asked, even though the answer was clear. He wanted to choke the life out of Nick, but his concern for Lori was the only thing keeping him from doing so. Drew rushed over to her side, which gave Nick just enough time to make a run for it. All the disarray caused a crowd to form, and bystanders watched and pointed as Drew carried Lori out of the party in his arms.

Drew secured Lori in his passenger seat and drove back to her place. He remembered her address from the house-warming party and was in no need of directions. He knocked on the door a few times, but no one was home. Lori softly muttered that her mother was out of town and handed Drew her apartment key to unlock the door. Drew helped walk Lori to her room and handed her the wastebasket from the restroom in case she needed to hurl throughout the night. He felt bad leaving her drunk and all alone in an empty apartment, so he offered to sleep on the couch. "No, Drew, don't leave the room. What if I need you?" He was sure it was just the alcohol talking, but he fulfilled her request and grabbed a blanket and an extra pillow from her closet to make himself comfortable on the floor.

Drew laid on the floor, near the foot of Lori's bed and stared at the ceiling. The madness from earlier left him feeling bothered by how reckless Lori was, putting herself in such a dangerous situation. He thought to himself: what if he hadn't been at that party tonight? What would have happened to Lori if he had not been there? Just the thought of such unknown outcomes troubled him deeply.

Later that day, Drew took Lori to Milo's Diner back in Huntley for lunch. The door chimed with each customer walking in and out of the store. When the waitress came to their table, Drew ordered two vanilla milkshakes. Drew spared no details of the attempted assault on her and suggested filing a police report, but she declined. She would rather not get the police involved and have to explain to her parents that she was out drinking at a frat house with college boys.

"You could've been raped! College guys are pigs; everyone knows that," Drew lectured Lori, like an upset parent watching their child spiral out of control. His concern for her was bolstering. As Drew's lips yammered on, Lori realized that her fondness for him was still present. Seeing how worried he was for her brought back old feelings.

"Lori, why did you break up with me? What are you so afraid of?"

"I'm afraid of ending up like my mom and dad. I'm afraid that if we eventually get married and have kids, you'll resent me for having a career and I'll resent you for not supporting me. I just don't want to end up like my parents" Lori elaborated how she projected those fears on her own relationship after internalizing the trauma she acquired from watching her parents.

Drew assured her, "You can't let that hold us back. I don't plan on getting married until way after college. There is no rush, we can take our time and figure out what we want."

"I'm sorry, Drew. I was so stupid." Lori declared, relieved that she and Drew finally had this heart-to-heart and were back on the same page.

On their way out of the diner, Lori heard an annoyingly recognizable voice say, "Ruth, I heard the most delicious piece of gossip." It was Barbara Ross, eager to spread the latest rumors in another booth.

"Oh, tell me more." The other woman said.

"I heard that mutinous Diane Sutton was sent to a nut-house back in May." Barbara explained.

The other woman chimed in, "Not surprising. I suppose it was only a matter of time until she got sent away."

"What a lunatic!" Barbara said while cackling with glee.

It was taunting for Lori to know that the scandalmongers of Huntley were still running their mouths about her mother's private business after everything she had been through over the past six months. Drew caught wind of the rumors and did his best to encourage Lori to ignore their nasty comments. Lori felt the overwhelming need to defend her mother's reputation and decided to give Barbara a piece of her mind.

"You love to gossip, but I don't think you can handle what people say behind your back," Lori interjected. "Do you even know what people say about you, Barbara? They say you're a dreadful bitch who's far too involved in people's personal lives."

Barbara clenched the pearls around her neck and retorted in shock, "You disrespectful little brat! Who do you think you are?"

Lori figured when it came to people like Barbara, the only way to get a point across was to stoop to their level. Drew took Lori by the shoulders and guided her out of the establishment, while Barbara stood fuming with anger, yelling out some choice words. Even Barbara's profanity couldn't stop Lori from walking out with her head held high.

Sunday, August 17th was day 3 of Woodstock, and it was just as eventful as the day before. John Sebastian, Grateful Dead, and Janis Joplin were among the popular names that rocked the crowd from Saturday into the early hours of Sunday morning. They wrapped up around 11 a.m. and took a smaller plane to New York City. While in the city, they seized the opportunity to explore the exciting borough of Manhattan. There, they visited the breathtaking Statue of Liberty, picnicked in Central Park, and caught a show on Broadway. They took advantage of the endless activities at their disposal as they frolicked through the sleepless streets of Times Square.

After Diane put the final touches on the article, Bruce insisted they go out to dinner to celebrate the successful completion of their news story. She rummaged through her wardrobe and agonized over what to wear. Suddenly, she noticed everything that was wrong with her body. She cringed at the mild stretch marks around her waist from when she carried Lori and a couple of gray hairs poking out of her scalp. She spruced herself up as best as she could for a middle-aged mother on the verge of divorce and sprayed on some perfume before heading out the door.

Bruce made reservations at a fancy restaurant in SoHo. He gifted her with a bouquet of yellow tulips. "Bruce, these are gorgeous," she exclaimed, stunned by the vibrant arrangements. He held the door open for her as she passed through and pulled out her chair before she sat down. They dined on succulent filet mignon, twice-baked potatoes topped with cheese and sour cream, and shared a mouthwatering crème brûlée for dessert. "Consider this your first business trip," he stated before toasting Diane with a glass of champagne. The pair chatted light-heartedly before the conversation became more serious.

"I'm getting divorced," she awkwardly announced, not sure when would have been the right time to mention it.

"Really? So, you finally decided to leave your husband, huh?" He responded to her unexpected statement.

"Actually, he initiated the divorce."

Bruce scoffed without saying a word, in an effort not to offend Diane with his honest opinion.

"What? Say what's on your mind Bruce."

"With all due respect Diane, from what I've heard, I don't think your husband ever truly loved you. He put you through hell for years, then turns around and divorces you for lashing out one time. The man is a coward."

"My mother said he was probably coming on so strong because I was 'emasculating' him. I spent so much of my life being a stay-at-home mom, he just couldn't handle it when I started working."

"That's no excuse. A real man isn't threatened by a strong woman. A real man is confident enough to let his woman shine and live up to her full potential. You are caring, intelligent, and you constantly put the needs of others before your own. A woman like you deserves the world, and its time you stop settling for anything less than that," he said, spoiling her with compliments.

Diane silently looked at him from across the table and wondered how someone so perfect was not yet taken.

After dinner, they returned to Bruce's hotel room. "Ugh, my feet are killing me," Diane whined as he led her to the couch. She took a seat before Bruce slipped off her shoes and rested one of her legs on his lap as he treated her to a celebratory foot rub. His charming wit and gentlemanly behavior only complemented his infectious charisma. Diane could no longer deny her attraction to Bruce; she was beginning to find him irresistible. In a smooth voice, he proceeded to bring up social topics as they shared their opinions about the world they lived in and ideas on how people could make it a better place.

"Maybe we could do this again sometime."

"Spend the weekend in a hotel room? You are aware that I am still technically married, right?"

"It's only a matter of time, and I don't mind waiting," Bruce flirted shamelessly. He had always found Diane attractive, but something about her was particularly sexy today. Bruce hit a spot on the ball of her foot that made her jump. She glanced over at a clock on the wall, reminding her it was time to head back to her room across the hall. She pulled her foot away from him and said her goodbyes.

"It has been a pleasure; goodnight, Bruce."

"Goodnight. In all seriousness, you did a great job today." Bruce opened his arms, and Diane walked into his embrace.

They hugged for a while, and the hug should have ended there, but it felt as if some kind of magnetic pull was yanking them closer together. His hands slipped down to the nape of her back. As he brought his face closer to hers, he could smell the mint on her breath from the gum she had been chewing earlier. She looked up at Bruce, who towered eight inches above her, and their eyes met. He cradled her face and kissed her. It started off slow; her lips met his, and his tongue rolled around in her mouth. He nibbled on her ear and bit her neck until her insides became moist with arousal. She realized things were going too far and pushed him away.

"Bruce, stop."

"I'm sorry. I just really wanted to kiss you."

"I really should go." Diane quickly put her shoes back on and bolted out of his room and back to hers.

"Shit," he said under his breath while rubbing the back of his head.

Bruce's heart was beating out of his chest as he ruminated over the line he had just crossed. What was he thinking, kissing a married woman? He suddenly heard a few knocks on his door and was surprised to see Diane on the opposite side when he opened it. She leapt into his arms, no longer able to fight the allure of spending the night with him.

After they ripped each other's clothes off, Bruce effortlessly hoisted her up onto the wooden dresser and briefly suckled on her neck before parting her legs. Diane's eyes rolled back in ecstasy as her breasts heaved with each thrusting motion; she felt herself getting closer to climax. His hand gently grazed her back and he noticed her scar, but she saved the explanation of that mark for another occasion.

Heat was building up underneath the thin hotel bed sheets. Beads of sweat began to form on Bruce's forehead as he put in an honest hour of work on Diane. Her moans of passion nearly woke the guests in the next room over. When they finally exhausted themselves, they laid side by side, breathing heavily before falling asleep in each other's arms.

Monday, August 18th, 1969, Diane woke up and started to think she should not have let that third glass of champagne from last night cloud her judgment completely. Just thinking about last night got her juices flowing all over again. She recalled the events from the night before that made her body quiver with ecstasy, all leading up to a mind-blowing orgasm. Still love-drunk from the sex last night, she became enamored with the idea of spending every second of the day together. Although her infatuation with Bruce was budding, she pumped the brakes on her compulsive emotions. The ink wasn't even dry on her divorce yet and the last thing she needed was to jump into a new relationship.

This business trip turned out to be the most romantic weekend of her life. Bruce showed her how to live, rather than just existing. A part of her felt guilty for spending the night with Bruce while her divorce was still in process, but she had to face the fact that her marriage was over. Her affection for Frank was depleting and shriveling up into only a handful of happy memories like their wedding day, Lori's first steps, and when Frank got that big promotion at work. She wished she could bottle up that happiness from those moments and consume that joy when hard times hit, but that simply wasn't possible.

Bruce and Diane got up and dressed just in time to catch their flight. When they landed back in Chicago before parting ways at the airport, he took her by the hand and asked how the night before would affect their relationship moving forward.

"I'm just not ready for a romantic relationship, Bruce. We work together and Lori's still adjusting to my separation from Frank. I'm not looking for anything serious right now." She explained.

"I understand, you have a lot on your plate right now. Just promise to give me a call when you are ready to get serious."

"I promise," Diane vowed.

Lori woke up to the sound of keys jingling in the door handle. She arose slowly, nearly forgetting that Drew had spent the night again and overslept. Diane's voice echoed,

"Morning Lori, I'm home." Lori gasped in shock; she wasn't expecting her mother to be back so soon. She shook Drew awake, told him to get dressed, and snuck him out through the fire escape before her mother could notice.

After Diane settled her bags into the apartment, she made sure to sit Lori down and describe the status of her terminal relationship with Frank. "Your father and I are getting divorced. I don't want you to feel like you have to pick sides. Frank may have done some awful things, but he is still your father, and he deserves your respect. However, as a woman, I don't ever want to see you in a situation like mine, so go to college and get your education. Make your own money so a man doesn't have the power to take it away from you, and remember that you are capable of being so much more than just someone's wife."

Those words resonated with Lori. She felt like she was getting a passionate speech from a profound female influencer like Eleanor Roosevelt or Gloria Steinem, but it was just her mother, and that made it even more impactful. As Lori's relationship with her mother flourished, Diane blossomed into the type of powerful female figure Lori looked up to.

Later that same night, Diane received a phone call.

"Hello," she said, not sure who could possibly be calling at this hour.

"Hell-- hello." It was Frank, slurring his words on the other line.

"Frank? Is that you?"

"Yes, it's me."

"You're drunk. Why are you calling me?" she asked, agitated that her snooze was being interrupted by these shenanigans.

"Diane, Diane, Diane. You were always playing the victim and making me out to be the bad guy. Do you really think you're the only one that was unhappy? I wasn't happy either, but at least I didn't spend all day crying about it."

"What are you talking about?" Diane asked, to get some clarification on why Frank was going on a drunken rant.

Frank finally spoke his truth and revealed a gripping explanation of some challenges he faced long before he even met Diane. Frank opened up about the night his father, Lieutenant Gerald Sutton, heard from neighbors that Frank was caught fraternizing with a young lady from the area. As it turns out, Sylvia Johnson had captured Frank's attention since they first met at the tender age of 17, but she was a negro, and the thought of Frank in an interracial relationship with a black woman disgusted his father.

Gerald, who was a raging alcoholic at the time, was furious and confronted Frank by attempting to throw him off the 6th-floor balcony of their apartment if he continued to see the "nigger girl" again. It was as if Frank could hear his father's voice all over again, forbidding him from seeing Sylvia, and threatening to kill Frank if he dishonored his family by dating outside of his race. After being forced to desert his desires, Frank followed in his father's footsteps and served a couple of years in the military before eventually settling down with Diane, whom he met after her senior year of high school. His relationship with Diane got Gerald's stamp of approval; after all, she was young, she came from a good family, and most importantly, she was white.

Frank had to accept that the world he lived in was not ready to embrace the love he had for Sylvia and would have never forgiven himself if any harm had ever come to her because of their relationship. When Frank's father died, that was one less major roadblock in the way of their love, but by then, it was too late; he had already established a life and family with Diane. What kind of man would he be if he ran out on his wife and child for another woman? So he stayed and continued on in his marriage, seeking Sylvia in secrecy a few times a year.

"Is that why you were always so cruel to me? Were you just taking out your anger on me because you couldn't be with the woman you really wanted?"

"Of course, it is Diane," Frank said before taking a pause to guzzle more alcohol in between his sentences.

"I've always felt like you resented me and this marriage."

It was as if all of the pieces to this puzzle were finally coming together. This was making so much more sense now, their entire marriage was built on a lie. Thus, they could never be truly happy. On some level, that conversation with Frank was enlightening and gave her some closure. She could finally stop blaming herself for the collapse of her marriage and forgive Frank for all the pain he caused her over the years. She never would have guessed that the deep-rooted issues Frank had were set in motion by his father all those years ago.

On December 4th, 1969, news broke that the FBI had been investigating the Black Panther party since their formation. Direct orders were given by the head of the FBI to assassinate Fred Hampton and as many members of the

Black Panther as possible, shamelessly proving that there was nothing America feared more than Black unity. Racist suspicion of a group that only sought unity and fair treatment caused the media to manufacture negative assumptions and label the group as "vicious" and "extremely dangerous", although there was no evidence to back up those accusations.

And so America was at the edge of its seat, constantly anticipating the worst from the Black Panthers, petrified that they would strike back and repay the United States for the atrocities this land had committed against them, their peers and their ancestors. The FBI grew more anxious and hostile at what the Black Panthers might do next and finally, took swift and violently lethal action by infiltrating the apartment building Fred was staying at and shooting into the unit.

After the raid, a total two people were dead: Fred Hampton and Mark Clark, co-leader of the Black Panthers, while several more panther members were seriously injured. This event had to be the most sickening display of egregiously unwarranted fear and paranoia fueled by racism Diane had ever seen. It turned her stomach to see that in the same year, the country had advanced enough to put man on the moon, yet the same government remained barbaric

111

enough to execute Fred Hampton and Mark Clark the way that it did. Knowing these disturbing truths about the world she lived in made Frank's decision to follow his father's orders so much more understandable. She could only imagine the kind obstacles Frank would have faced had he pursued an interracial relationship with Sylvia twenty-five years ago.

As time marched on, Diane became a sensational journalist. Her success had taken her far beyond the Chicago Tribune; she went on to cover national stories and interviewed public figures, political leaders, and celebrities. She traveled the world and experienced things that may not have been possible living out her existence as a housewife.

One evening after work, Diane arrived at the new home she recently purchased. Earlier that week, she spoke to Lori, who was now a student at the University of Chicago, majoring in behavioral health. Diane skimmed through the mail on the kitchen counter and found a letter from the courthouse that was made out to her. She opened the notice, and it stated that after two years of being legally separated, her divorce was now officially finalized. As for Frank, he had moved to Milwaukee to be in a relationship with Sylvia. They are expecting a baby boy. Last Diane heard, Frank was getting help for his drinking and anger management. She was surprisingly supportive and happy to know that Frank was finally living for himself, as was she.

She grabbed the telephone and began to dial a familiar number.

"Hello, Bruce, it's Diane. Are you free next weekend?" She asked with a smirk, finally ready to entertain the idea of a new love interest.

~The End~